This motivational journal belongs to:

Copyright © 2024 by Benito Serna Jr.

All rights reserved. No part of this publication may be reproduced, distributed, or transmitted in any form or by any means, including photocopying, recording, digital scanning, or other electronic or mechanical methods, without the prior written permission of the publisher, except in the case of brief quotation embodied in critical reviews and certain other noncommercial uses permitted by copyright law. For permission requests, please address Holzer Books LLC.

Published 2024
Printed in the United States of America

First Edition
ISBN (softcover): 978-1-963380-11-8
ISBN (hardcover): 978-1-963380-12-5

For information, address:
Holzer Books LLC
8 The Green, Ste. A
Dover, Delaware 19901 USA

For information about special discounts available for bulk purchases, sales promotions, and educational needs, contact:
info@holzerbooksllc.com
+1 (888) 901-7776

CREED OF A LEADER

by BENNY SERNA

I take calculated risks.

I live and think outside the box.

I am the example.

I trust my instinct.

I believe in myself.

I state the facts free
from my personal opinion.

I never compromise my integrity.

I have the power of influence and
I use it to improve those I lead.

I exceed all expectations.

I envision my goals daily.

I am not afraid of making decisions.

I don't look back.

I am not afraid to fail.

I speak with purpose.

I am committed.

I never give up.

I am a Leader.

I take calculated risks.

I live and think outside the box.

I am the example.

I trust my instinct.

I believe in myself.

I state the facts free from my personal opinion.

I never compromise my integrity.

I have the power of influence and I use it to improve those I lead.

I exceed all expectations.

I envision my goals daily.

I am not afraid of making decisions.

I don't look back.

I am not afraid to fail.

I speak with purpose.

I am committed.

I never give up.

I take calculated risks.

I live and think outside the box.

I am the example.

I trust my instinct.

I believe in myself.

I state the facts free from my personal opinion.

I never compromise my integrity.

I have the power of influence and I use it to improve those I lead.

I exceed all expectations.

I envision my goals daily.

I am not afraid of making decisions.

I don't look back.

I am not afraid to fail.

I speak with purpose.

I am committed.

I never give up.

I am a leader.

I take calculated risks.

I live and think outside the box.

I am the example.

I trust my instinct.

I believe in myself.

I state the facts free from my personal opinion.

I never compromise my integrity.

I have the power of influence and I use it to improve those I lead.

I exceed all expectations.

I envision my goals daily.

I am not afraid of making decisions.

I don't look back.

I am not afraid to fail.

I speak with purpose.

I am committed.

I never give up.

I am a leader.

I take calculated risks.

I live and think outside the box.

I am the example.

I trust my instinct.

I believe in myself.

I state the facts free from my personal opinion.

I never compromise my integrity.

I have the power of influence and I use it to improve those I lead.

I exceed all expectations.

I envision my goals daily.

I am not afraid of making decisions.

I don't look back.

I am not afraid to fail.

I speak with purpose.

I am committed.

I never give up.

I am a leader.

I take calculated risks.

I live and think outside the box.

I am the example.

I trust my instinct.

I believe in myself.

I state the facts free from my personal opinion.

I never compromise my integrity.

I have the power of influence and I use it to improve those I lead.

I exceed all expectations.

I envision my goals daily.

I am not afraid of making decisions.

I don't look back.

I am not afraid to fail.

I speak with purpose.

I am committed.

I never give up.

I take calculated risks.

I live and think outside the box.

I am the example.

I trust my instinct.

I believe in myself.

I state the facts free from my personal opinion.

I never compromise my integrity.

I have the power of influence and I use it to improve those I lead.

I exceed all expectations.

I envision my goals daily.

I am not afraid of making decisions.

I don't look back.

I am not afraid to fail.

I speak with purpose.

I am committed.

I never give up.

I am a leader.

I take calculated risks.

I live and think outside the box.

I am the example.

I trust my instinct.

I state the facts free from my personal opinion.

I never compromise my integrity.

I have the power of influence and I use it to improve those I lead.

I exceed all expectations.

I envision my goals daily.

I am not afraid of making decisions.

I don't look back.

I am not afraid to fail.

I speak with purpose.

I never give up.

Made in United States
Troutdale, OR
11/03/2026

56845369R00070